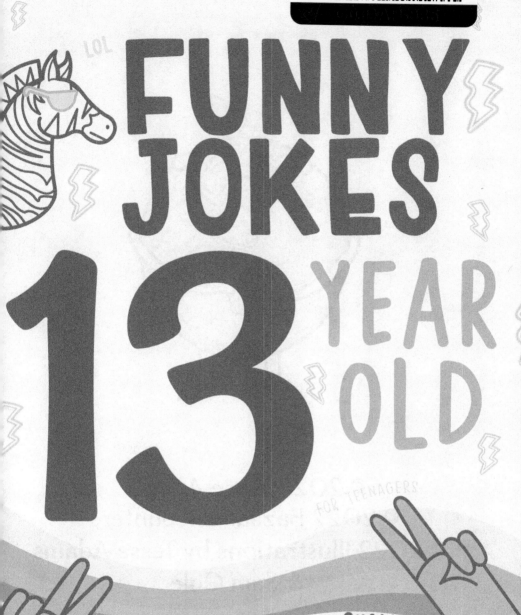

FUNNY JOKES

13 YEAR OLD

DARE YOU NOT TO LAUGH CHALLENGE

Totally Awesome Joke Book for Teens

1

3

My dad asked me when my midterm exam was. I said, "March 1st."

So he walked around the room and asked again.

Stop pulling my leg!

ha-ha
[hah-hah] phrase.

I really don't think it's funny,
but I want to stay on your good side.

What rock group has four guys who don't sing?

Mount Rushmore!

Why don't crabs give to charity?

Because they're SHELL-fish.

Why does Harry Styles play baseball?

Because he has perfect PITCH!

Beware of your shadow.

It's acting SHADY!

What do you call a fake pasta?

An impasta!

Why did the clock get kicked out
of class?

It TOCKED too much!

What do you call a motor with ears?

An ENGINEER.

What is the best website to find information about a DJ?

Wiki-wiki-wiki-pedia.

Why doesn't Mario use the internet?

He is afraid of the BROWSERS!

Why shouldn't you bother talking about fashion?

It goes in one YEAR and out the next.

Who is the worst gamer in the world?

Ezekiel!

Password reassures itself...
I am a strong and confident password,
Don't Listen to Google!

feet

[feet] noun.

Two sensitive devices used in finding Legos in the dark.

How do ghosts open doors?

With Spoo-KEYS!

When is homework not homework anymore?

When it is TURNED into a teacher!

Making a deep-dish pizza cake is really easy!

It's a PIZZA CAKE!

Where can you always find fame and fortune?

In the dictionary!

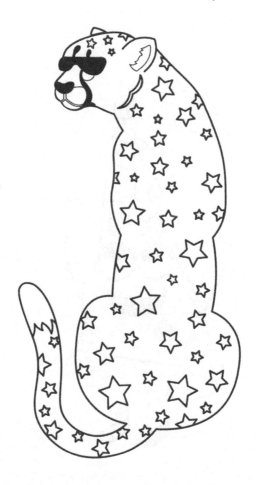

I am thinking about going into accounting when I go to college.

It's not a glam job, but it pays the bills.

Why don't vampires
attack Taylor Swift?

BAD BLOOD.

What do you call a hen who counts
her own eggs?

A mathemachicken!

Paintball may not improve your life.

But it's worth a SHOT!

When should you bring an umbrella
if you're headed for the kitchen?

When grandma is COOKING UP A STORM!

What do rainbows do in prison?

They REFRACT on what they
have done.

I PAUSED MY GAME TO BE HERE

textplanation
[tekst-spluh-ney-shuhn] noun.

I don't want to have a long phone conversation.

What do you call it when a chicken looks at her salad?

Chicken Caesar Salad.

I don't think I could handle a job on a submarine.

Too much PRESSURE.

A book of synonyms fell off the bookcase and landed on my head.

I had THESAURUS head ever... I guess I only have my SHELF to blame.

Teacher: Where can you find the Red Sea?

Student: Usually on my report card!

How much does a rainbow weigh?

It's actually PRETTY LIGHT.

What do call a magician who loses his magic?

Ian!

Why is Europe like a frying pan?

Because it has Greece on the bottom!

I took a pole recently and found that...

100% of the people in the tent
were upset.

I didn't want to play with my
friend on Minecraft... so I
BLOCKED him.

What did the alien say when it was time
to leave?

Gotta BLAST!

If Mario lived in the United States, what state would he live in?

Luigiana!

What does a millennial cowboy say?

YEET Haw!

What do boba teas say at an unexpected party?

SIP-rise!

I wanted to join the band, "Missing Dog."

You probably have seen
the posters.

Hi.
I don't care
Thanks.

Why don't vampires use autocorrect?

Because they love Type O's!

Did you hear about the new cheese movie?

It's G-RATED.

What is the most musical part of your body?

Your nose, you can blow it and pick it!

The flashlight on my phone broke.

Now I'm delighted.

Are balloon animals smart?

No, they are AIRHEADS!

My little brother doesn't know
what oblivious means.

He really has NO IDEA.

What is another word in the thesaurus for mother?

Can't say. MUMS the word.

What do you do if a teacher rolls her eyes at you?

Roll them back.

To the person who stole our front door welcome mat.

How LOW can you go?

How do computers attack each other?

By using pop-up ads.

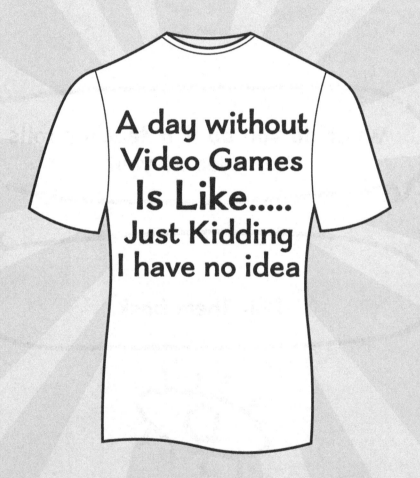

A day without
Video Games
Is Like.....
Just Kidding
I have no idea

What do snowmen do on vacation?

Chill Out.

Mom childproofed our house.

I'm not worried, I can still get in!

What's the leading cause of dry skin?

Towels.

Whiteboards are remarkable.

What did Ed Sheeran say when his speaker went up in flames?

I see fire!

What superhero asks too many questions?

Wonder woman!

Armed Robbery

What do you call a pirate who skips classes?

Captain Hooky.

DON'T RUSH ME,
I'M WAITING FOR
THE LAST MINUTE

Why won't Americans switch to
a dollar coin?

They're afraid of CHANGE.

Why can you always tell what the
Cat in the Hat will do next?

Because he is so easy to read.

Who keeps the tooth fairy busy?

Professional boxers.

What do you say when a kazoo player
sneezes?

KAZOONTITE!

Who doesn't like pizza?

Weird-DOUGHS!

My friend's Xbox, PS4, and Switch all broke on the same day.

He was inconsolable.

Snow White took six dwarfs to the orthodontist for braces.

None of them were HAPPY.

What kind of bull is the cutest?
A dor-a-BULL.

latte

[lah-tey] noun.

Italian for "a pricey coffee that gives you cavities."

I accidentally handed a glue stick to my friend instead of lip gloss.

She still isn't talking to me.

What's a space pirate's favorite planet?

mARRRRS!

Why did the forgetful teacher go for a run?

She wanted to JOG her memory!

Why does Bigfoot have a hairy coat?

FUR protection.

What did the ghost teacher say to the class?

Look at the board and I will go through it again!

What happens to zombies when it rains?

They get wet.

My brother switched the labels on the spice jars in our kitchen.

His THYME is CUMIN!

I was going to make a giraffe joke.

But it's too long.

Want to hear a joke about
cliffhangers...

Why haven't aliens visited our planet yet?

They read the reviews...only 1 star!

PULL YOURSELF TOGETHER MAN!

Friend 1: "Bro, can you pass me a pamplet?"
Friend 2: "Brochure."

I AM NOT
BOSSY
I JUST KNOW
WHAT YOU SHOULD
BE DOING

What kind of music do mummies listen to?

WRAP music!

y'all

[yawl] pronoun.

1. Used in addressing more than one person.
2. Used to address anything that needs a good talkin' to.

Why did the pig take a bath?

Because the farmer said, "Hogwash!"

What wizard is good at golf?

Harry PUTTER!

Why was the computer cold?

It left the WINDOWS open.

My dad thinks that I am obsessed with aliens from outer space.

What planet does he live on?

Did you hear about the guy who was fired at the dollar store?

He stopped making CENTS

What do you read to little zombies at night?

Deadtime stories.

Big Brother: "Why do you have a rubberband around your head?"

Little Brother: "I am trying to make SNAP decisions!"

Don't use goulash as a password.

It's not STROGANOFF!

Why shouldn't you write with a broken pencil?

Because it is POINTLESS!

Why don't mummies go on vacation?

They are afraid to UNWIND.

What kind of cheese causes trouble?

SHARP cheese.

What music scares balloon animals?

Pop music.

What kind of birthday cakes do they
have in heaven?

Angel cake.

What do elves do after school?

Their gnome-work.

Ladders can't be trusted.

They are always up to something.

How do you make a hot dog stand?

Take away its chair.

What do you call a teacher who doesn't fart in public?

A private TOOTor.

Just Googled "how to light a candle..."

got 10 million MATCHES.

What kind of cheese causes trouble?

SHARP cheese.

What do you call a paper airplane
that doesn't fly?

Stationary.

Why did the hipster burn his tongue?

He bit into his pizza before it
was COOL.

What do you call a police officer
that will not get out of bed?

An undercover cop.

How do you pay for a cow?

With MOOla.

**Accordion to science...
You can switch out words for
musical instruments, and a lot
of people won't notice.**

Knock, knock.
Who's there?
Hulu.
Hulu Who.

Why are zombies good at Minecraft?

DEAD-ication!

shower
[shou-er] noun.

The shortened term for
"personal concert hall"

Why did the smartphone need glasses?

It lost all its contacts.

Why did the phone go to the dentist?

It was having trouble with its Bluetooth!

What are the coolest books that you can read?

FAN fictions!

What kind of musical instrument
is always free?

An AIR GUITAR.

What do you call vegan headphones?

BEETS.

Student: " Would I be in trouble for
something that I didn't do?"

Teacher: "No, of course not."

Student: "Good, I didn't do my
homework."

I WENT
OUTSIDE ONCE,
THE GRAPHICS
WEREN'T
THAT GOOD.

What bus cannot bring you
to school?

A syllabus!

What kind of car can you drive
into deep water?

A Scubaru!

Don't worry about your computer
or your smartphone spying on you...
...your vacuum cleaner has been
gathering dirt on you for a long
time.

What do you have in December
that you don't have in any other
month?

D!

What do you call a fish with two knees?

A two-knee fish.

What do you call a jacket that
is on fire?

A BLAZER!

Friend 1: "I'm not sure what
cloning means."

Friend 2: "That makes two of us!"

I wanted to wear my camo shirt.

But I couldn't find it.

Why are toilets so good at poker?

They always get a FLUSH.

How much does it cost Santa
to land on the house?

"Nothing, it's on the house!"

Why do hamburgers love young
people?

Because they are PRO-TEEN.

What should you do when you
see a spaceman?

You just park it, man!

What is the definition of a farmer?

Someone who is good in their field.

Two illustrators were arguing about who was a better artist.

The argument ended in a DRAW.

Why couldn't the 13 year-old get into the pirate movie?

Because it was rated ARRRRR!

What's the difference between roast beef and pea soup?

Anyone can roast beef.

If you are a singer, don't yell into a colander...

you will STRAIN your voice.

Pooping jokes are not my favorite...

but they are a definite number two.

Why did the tortilla chip start dancing?

Because it dipped into the salsa!

Why are most bloggers good at geometry?

They know all the good ANGLES!

We used to call them "food fights"...

today we call the "all you can YEET buffets."

I've got your back!

Teacher: "You will never be successful because you procrastinate too much!"

Student: "Just you wait!"

What do you do if you are
addicted to seaweed?

Seek KELP.

Friend 1: "Do you want to play
a board game?"

Friend 2: "I'd rather play
a FUN game!"

What did the guitar say to
the ukuele?

Uke, I am your father.

I accidentally tasted my cat's food.

Don't ask MEOW.

There is a new rap song about
hand sanitizer.

It's fine. The lyrics are CLEAN.

If Apple made a car... would
it have windows?

What do porcupine fish say when
they kiss?

OUCH!

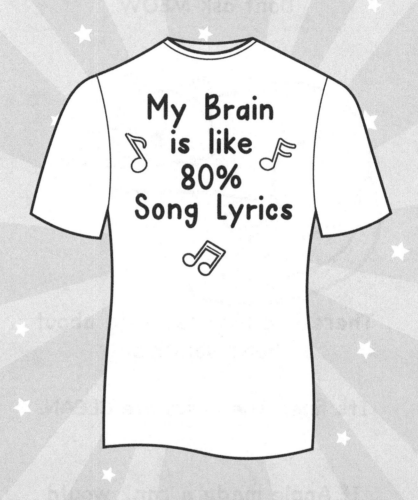

My Brain
is like
80%
Song Lyrics

You really got to hand it to the
short people out there.

Seriously, they can't reach it.

Sad spelled backwards is Das.

Das is not good.

My sister is starting her new job
at a restaurant tomorrow.

She can't WAIT.

We have enough youth...

how about a fountain of money.

What kind of shoes do ninjas wear?

SNEAKers.

What do you call a wizard with
wireless headphones?

AIRY PODDER.

Teacher: "It's very muggy out today"

Student: "I don't see any mugs."

What do you call someone whose job it is to separate fact from fiction?

A librarian.

Teacher: "What do you call a teacher without pupils?"

Student: "Blind."

Long fairy tales...

Seem to DRAGON.

What is E.T. short for?

Because he has little legs.

You know, people say they pick their nose...?

I feel like I was just born with mine.

What is the most popular craft for teens?

Minecraft!

Giraffes are such snobs.

They look down on everyone.

What sport can you play on a carpet?

RUGby!

NOT A HUGGER

What is the collective noun for a group of cars?

A lot.

We lost power for a whole week last year.

Those were the DARKEST days of my life.

What do you call a boat that is 10% off?

A SALE boat.

Who is the smartest mountain?

Mount CLEVERest.

What did the irratated gardener say?

"What in CARNATION!"

What do you call a laughing motorcycle?

A YAMAHAHAHA.

I wrote a song about tortillas.

Come to think of it, it's actually more of a WRAP.

Have you ever let out a huge sigh of relief when you find your lost phone?

Only a PHEW will understand.

To the person who stole my place in line. I'm after you now.

What do you call a lazy baby
kangaroo?

A pouch potato.

Mom wanted me to clear
the dinner table.

I needed a RUNNING START,
but I made it!

Who is the poorest rapper?

50 cent.

Don't swallow food coloring.

**The nurse said I may feel BLUE
for a few days.**

NOPE.

**What do you call an elephant
that is good at yoga?**

A liar.

Did you hear the joke about the toilet?

Never mind, it STINKS.

Friend 1: "Why are you staring at that orange juice container?"

Friend 2: "It says CONCENTRATE!"

Why was the Queen only 12 inches tall?

Because she was the RULER.

What is the worst kind of cat to have?

A CATastrophe!

Have you heard about the movie, Constipation?

That's because it hasn't come out yet.

Don't go to a seafood disco.

You might pull a MUSSEL.

I recently heard a bad food joke.

It was hard to DIGEST.

Don't you just love the way the Earth rotates around the sun?

It really makes my day.

Why can't you trust your bed?

It's always lying behind you.

Never work at a peanut butter factory.

They are all nuts.

What sport are ranchers good at?

Fencing.

What do you call a herd of sheep falling down a hill?

A LAMBslide.

They all say that "money talks"...

But all mine says to me is "goodbye!"

I saw an ad that said, "iphone for sale, volume stuck on high, for $1."

I thought to myself, I can't turn that down.

Well, that's not a good sign.

What kind of photos do elves take?

Elfies.

Why are cemeteries so noisy?

Because of all the COFFIN.

Bicycles cannot stand on their own,
they're two tired.

What has 40 feet and sings?

The school choir.

Why is bread lots of fun?

Because it's made of WHEEEEE-at!

Do you have holes in your underwear?

No? So how do you put your legs
through?

Where does T-rex go shopping?

At the dino store.

Why did the farmer become a DJ?

Because he had SICK BEETS.

It's fun to tell jokes about the Rolling Stones.

In fact, it's a gas, gas, gas.

I have a great joke about nepotism.

But I only share it with my family.

Did you hear about the famous pickle?

He is a big DILL!

Ohhhhhh...

[ohhhhh] phrase.

I still don't get it.

Why do astronomers put beef in their soap?

For meatier showers.

I FOUND
THIS
ON MY
FLOORDROBE

What does a hamburger do for fun?

BUN-gee jumping!

Voldemort: "So...I just have to lie?"

Pinocchio: "Yep."

I informed my suitcases that we will not be going on vacation this year.

Now I'm dealing with EMOTIONAL BAGGAGE.

Why doesn't Spongebob have a holiday like his friend?

Saint Patrick's Day...

Dad grilled a chicken for 4 hours.

We still don't know why it crossed the road.

**Thanks for explaining the word "umpteen" to me...
It means A LOT.**

When is a tire a bad singer?

When it's FLAT.

What food has a lot of money?

FORTUNE cookies.

Why shouldn't you tell a secret
in front of a clock?

Because time will tell!

What time is it when 10 zombies
are chasing you?

Ten after one!

Why didn't the hyena cross the road?

It was too busy laughing.

We threw a house-warming
party for our Eskimo friend.

Sadly, he is homeless now.

How do you make a fruit roll?

You push it!

What do you call it when a ghost scares you over and over again?

Deja-BOO!

What do you call a man who has finished digging a hole?

Doug.

What animal asks too many questions?

A WHY-nocerous!

What has two legs, but cannot walk?

A pair of pants!

How long is "just a minute?"

That depends on what side of the bathroom door you're on.

It would be cool if Netflix made a show about Area 51.

Well, Stranger Things have happened!

What did the baby corn say to the mama corn?

"Where's Popcorn?"

Librarians are too strict...

they always go by the book.

What do you call a movie that has Tom Cruise and a hamburger in it?

Top BUN.

Genie: What is your third wish?

Boy: I wish I had a double.

Geniie: Weiird wiish, but okay.

What monster fits on the tip of your finger?

The bogeyman.

Why couldn't the laptop take
off his hat?

He had the CAPS LOCK on.

Witches don't fart.

They cast SMELLS!

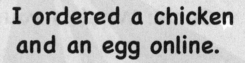

I ordered a chicken
and an egg online.

I'll let you know.

Why did the nose stay home from
school?

It was being picked on.

How does a hamburger introduce
his girlfriend?

Meat Patty.

SARCASTIC COMMENT
LOADING

PLEASE WAIT...

What do you call an average potato?

A commontater.

Where do kangaroo dads fart?

OUT-BACK.

teenager
[teen-ey-jer] noun.

A person who is better prepared for a zombie apocalypse than for school tomorrow.

What do you get when you cross
a wolf with a sheep?

A wolf.

Where do ghosts live?

BOO York!

Why did the drummer go to
bed early?

He was BEAT.

What's the opposite of a mermaid?

Landlady.

What do you call a werewolf that's not hiding?

Therewolf!

What were the lion and the witch doing in the wardrobe?

Narnia business!

How do wizards write?

In CURSIVE!

How does a baby look something up on the computer?

They "GOO GOO" it!

Why do cats have bad breath?

They use MOUSE-wash.

Two ghosts got married and had a family.

The kids aren't much to look at.

Why doesn't the cat get to use her computer?

Because she's too busy playing with the mouse.

I want to put horns on my laptop.

It will improve its RAM capability.

What kind of keys are sweet?

Cookies.

How much does it cost Santa to fly around the world on Christmas Eve?

Eight BUCKS, sometimes nine.

I like to press the F5 key after a long day at school...

It is so REFRESHING.

I had an out-of-body experience today.

I was beside myself.

What is a ghost's favorite fruit?

BOOnanas!

Friend 1: I am going to put Instagram on my phone.

Friend 2: That's nice that you are putting your Grandma on speed dial.

Knock, knock.
Who's there?
Britney Spears.
Britney Spears who?
Knock, knock.
Who's there?
Oops! I did it again.

If I refuse to go to gym class...

Is that resistance training?

Friend 1: Is this pool safe for diving?

Friend 2: It deep ends.

Why shouldn't you eat joke books?

Because they would taste funny!

You should say thank you to all the sidewalks out there...

for keeping us off the streets.

I asked my dad if I could go to a 50 Cent concert.

He gave me $2.00 and told me to bring a few friends!

My little sister couldn't figure
out the seatbelt.

Then it clicked.

What did the skunk say when the
wind changed direction?

"It's all coming back to me now."

Why does the landlord let 9
ants live in his apartment for free?

Because they aren't TEN-ANTS!

Today my friend ate 77 french fries.

That's ODD.

I accidentally spilled apple juice
on my smartphone.

It was a CIDER attack.

Starbucks messed up my coffee
order again, so they gave me
a free coffee.

Thanks a latte.

I'm really into condiments on my food...

in fact, I RELISH it.

I HAD MY
Patience
TESTED
≥I'M≤
negative

Do you think jellyfish are sad
because there are no peanut
butterfish?

What are caterpillars afraid of?

DOG-erpillars?

You are in a room with walls made of steel, and no windows or doors. All you have is a computer. How do you get out?

Press the escape key.

If a mitochondria could take it's own photo...
would it be called a CELLfie?

Don't kiss anyone if you have a runny nose.
You might think it's funny...
but it's SNOT.

If you see an Apple store
robbery...

Does that make you an iWitness?

I just found out that Canada
isn't real.

Turns out it was all MAPLE LEAF.

HOLD ON.

I SEE A DOG

What do you call an empty can
of Cheez Whiz?

Cheez Was.

Friend 1: Do you want to go
to yoga class with me?

Friend 2: Namaste here.

The ice cream truck is charging
$10 for popsicles.

That isn't COOL.

from mom & dad gift tag

[fruhm mom & dad gift tag] phrase.

Dad is just as surprised as you are.

What do you call a DJ on Halloween?

The BOOGIE-MAN!

Did you hear about the new restaurant on the moon?

Great food, no atmosphere.

What do you call a lonely cheese?

Prov-alone.

It took me 11 puns to get my friend to laugh...

because no pun in ten did.

You can't plant a vegetable garden...

If you haven't BOTANY seeds.

Mom says I have two faults: I don't listen and something else.

What is orange and sounds like a parrot?

A carrot!

What is the best way to get attention from your dad?

Sit down and look comfortable.

What did the lawyer name his daughter?

Sue.

This is Bob.
Bob has no arms.

"Knock, knock."
"Who is it?"
"It isn't Bob."

Don't try to have a conversation
on a carousel ride...

...you will just talk
in circles.

home
[hohm] noun.

Where my video games live
and are always there for me

I burnt my Hawaiian pizza.

I guess I should have put it on ALOHA temperature.

What did the hostile cake say?

"You want a piece of me?"

Why the long face?

Books From Tesse Adams.
More Ages Coming Soon!

Made in the USA
Las Vegas, NV
23 February 2024

86187988R00066